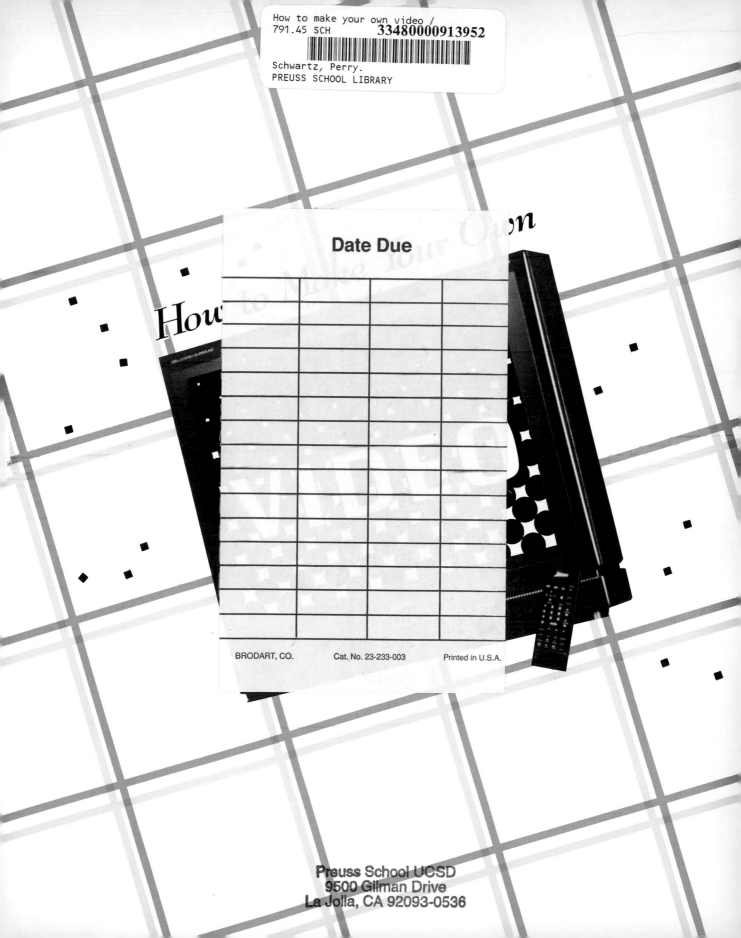

MEDIA WORKSHOP

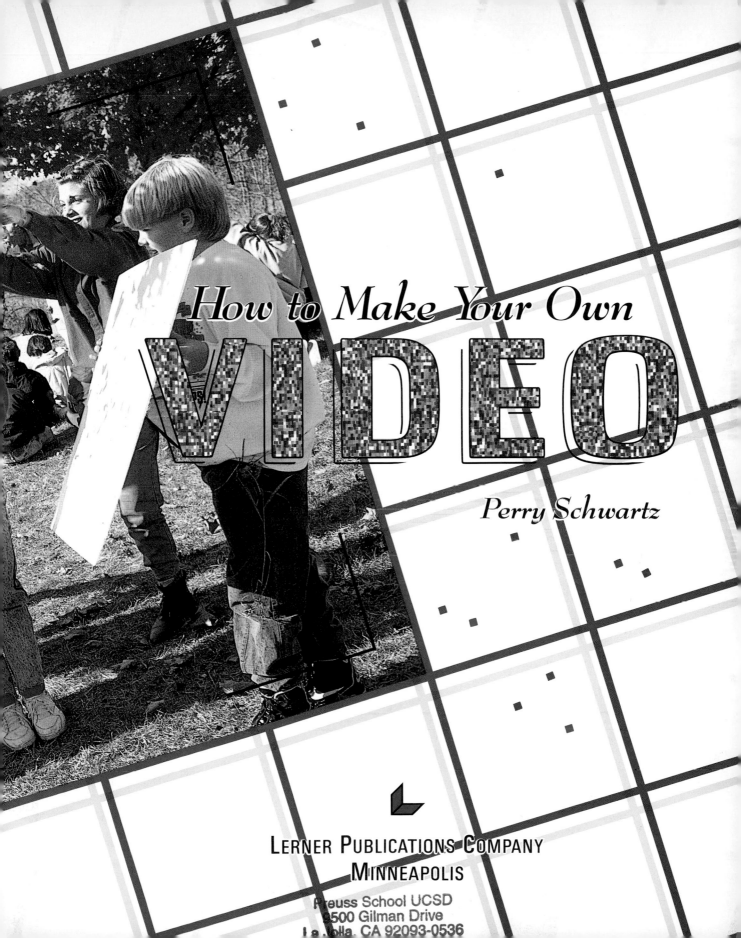

How to Make Your Own
VIDEO

Perry Schwartz

LERNER PUBLICATIONS COMPANY
MINNEAPOLIS

Acknowledgments

Many people deserve recognition and thanks for helping with this book. In particular, I would like to thank Ms. Martha Mason, teacher at Alice Smith Elementary School, who was so helpful in organizing the picture-taking event, our naturalist, Mr. Jim Gilbert, photographer David Boe, the Lowry Nature Center at Carver Park, and all the kids who helped make the pictures possible: Steve Braun, Angela Conklin, Lee Lovering, David Olson, Meghan Robinson, Clara Schroedl, Voradeth Thatsanaphone, and Jenny Uglem.

The photographs and illustrations in this book are reproduced courtesy of: Zenith Electronics Corp., pp. 1, 69; David Boe, pp. 2-3, 4, 8, 10, 11, 12, 13, 14, 16, 18, 20, 21 (top, middle), 22, 26 (left), 30, 36, 37, 38, 39, 40, 41, 42, 43, 44, 47, 48, 49, 52, 53, 54, 55, 63, 64, 65, 66; L. Engfer, pp. 21 (bottom), 26 (right); K. Sirvaitis, p. 23 (top); Laura Westlund, pp. 23 (bottom), 34, 41, 45, 50 (inset), 52 (top), 56, 58, 67; Coors Brewing Co., p. 25; Atlanta Convention and Visitors Bureau, p. 45; North Carolina Travel and Tourism Div., p. 50; Charley Murphy, p. 67; Ampex Corp., p. 68; KHOP-TV, Hopkins School District, p. 70.

The cover photographs are by David Boe. Digitization by Charley Murphy.

This book is available in two editions:
Library binding by Lerner Publications Company
Soft cover by First Avenue Editions
241 First Avenue North/Minneapolis, MN 55401
ISBN 0-8225-2301-9 (lib. bdg.)/ISBN 0-8225-9588-5 (pbk.)

Schwartz, Perry.
    How to make your own video / Perry Schwartz.
        p.   cm.
    Includes index.
    Summary: Covers all the technical basics of making a camcorder home video, and focuses especially on elements of production, direction, and creative use of subjects and scripts.
    ISBN 0-8225-2301-9
    1. Video tape recorders and recording—Juvenile literature.
2. Video recordings—Production and direction—Juvenile literature.
[1. Video tape recorders and recording. 2. Video recordings—
—Production and direction.] I. Title.
TK6655.V5S38   1991   90-24531
791.45'023—dc20   CIP
                                              AC

Manufactured in the United States of America

········ Contents ········

• • • • • • • • • • • • • • • • •

This book is dedicated to Catherine, Elizabeth, Carolyn, and Michael, all of whom have taught me to see.

YOU MUST FIRST HAVE SOMETHING TO SAY

Many books, articles, and even videos on the subject of videomaking begin with what appears to be the obvious: how to operate a camcorder. They offer tips on how to hold the camera, how to use the auto focus, and how to understand the auto iris.

This book is different. Its premise is that the most important thing about making a video is to have something to say and to know how to say it. A good story well told is the key to making a good video, whether it's a simple school project or a $50 million Hollywood epic.

To be sure, technical issues are important.

If your video is so dark or out of focus that the audience can't see what's happening, or if the picture is so jerky that viewers get sick when they look at the screen, your video will not be successful. In this book you will learn the technical basics you need to know to make a good video.

Good technique, however, will not matter if you have no story, or if the story is told so poorly that it doesn't communicate or hold the audience's attention. Later in this book, we will discuss the elements of good storytelling. First, let's learn to see the way a camera sees.

The area inside the rectangle that the camcorder sees is called the frame. To change what is seen inside the frame, either the camcorder or the subject must be moved, to the left or right or closer or farther away. On most camcorders, you can accomplish this with a zoom lens.

Chapter One

SEE THE WAY A CAMERA SEES

A video camera—or any camera, for that matter—looks at the world quite differently from the way our eyes do. As a videomaker, it is important for you to learn to see the way a camera sees.

Peripheral Vision

Everything we see with our eyes (without turning our heads) is referred to as our *field of view*. Within our field of view, our eyes have peripheral vision; that is, they see things to the left and right as well as in the center. A camera cannot see out of the "corner" of its eye. It just sees what the lens is pointed at. The outer boundary of what the camera sees is called the **frame**. Anything outside the frame doesn't exist. We can only change the frame by moving the camera.

Focal Length

Our eyes create an image of the world in one size. To see more or less of something, we have to physically move away from or toward it. For example, if we stand at the base of a skyscraper, it would be difficult, if not impossible, to see the entire building. For our eyes to take in the whole building, we would have to move away from it. Conversely, if we want to see the detail in a faraway object, we must move closer to it.

Many camera lenses are built like our eyes—they create an image of only one size. The **focal length** of a lens indicates the size of the image the lens creates. Short focal length lenses create wide-angle images, and long focal length lenses, often called **telephoto** lenses, create large images of distant objects. To change the image size, we must move the camera or the object—unless we have a **zoom** lens. (More about the zoom lens in the next chapter.)

The focal length of all lenses is measured in millimeters, written as "mm." A 50mm lens is the most common lens, because it "sees" an image in a way that is similar to human vision. A 7mm lens—called a "fish-eye" because the glass bulges out like a fish's eye—is a very wide-angle lens that creates a distorted image, stretching and bending the object it sees. A 125mm lens is a telephoto lens. Each kind of lens creates a very different image of the same subject.

Notice the differences in these pictures of the same subject shot with three different lenses:
1) a 7mm fish-eye lens
2) a 50mm lens
3) a 125mm telephoto lens.

Camcorders do not record well in low light. Night scenes that might look fine to your eyes will likely be dark on your video. The photograph at left was taken with a still camera. A night scene taken by a camcorder (**inset**) is of much worse quality.

Gathering Light

The lenses in our eyes and camera lenses all gather light. Our brains present light to us in the form of an image that we see. A camera is the "brain" of the lens, but compared to the human brain, the camcorder is not a good recorder.

A scene that looks well lit to our eyes may look dark and dingy to a camcorder. This is especially true at night. On a beautiful, star-lit evening, with our eyes we can see not only the outlines of buildings, but detail as well. If we set up a camcorder to shoot the same scene, the resulting image would probably look as though we were shooting inside a dark tunnel. Hardly any of the information, let alone the detail that we can see with our eyes, can be seen by the camcorder. To compensate for the camera's poor recording abilities, we often have to help it see by adding more light than naturally exists.

Focusing and Depth of Field

Camera lenses, like human eyes, work to focus images so they appear sharp and clear. Working in cooperation with the brain, our eyes automatically refocus from a near object to a far object—they don't focus on everything in between. The camcorder can't refocus in quite the same way. It must be focused manually, or, with "auto focus" camcorders, by means of an infrared light beam. The camcorder will focus on everything that is in between the near and far object.

All lenses have a focus ring, such as the one to the right, that is marked in feet and meters. If you set the focus ring at 9 feet (3 meters), objects that are 9 feet away will be in sharpest focus in your picture. The distance between the nearest and

farthest objects in focus—the zone of sharp focus—is called **depth of field**. The depth of field in the example below is approximately 5 feet (1.5 m) in front of and behind Angela.

Depending on how much of the background and foreground is in focus, the depth of field is said to be shallow—only a small part of the image is in focus—or deep—close and faraway objects are all in focus.

Depth of field is controlled by changing the **aperture** setting, or lens opening. Changes in the aperture are controlled by the **iris**, a device inside the lens that makes the aperture smaller or larger, letting in more or less light, much like the pupil of an eye. Aperture sizes are measured in "f" numbers. Many lenses have f numbers from f2.8, the largest, to f22, the smallest. The smaller the number (such as f2.8), the more shallow the depth of field will be.

Selective focusing means to focus on one object so that the rest of the objects in the frame are out of focus. Selective focusing directs the audience's attention to a certain point.

Above: Selective focusing helps call attention to one part of a scene. **Below:** The depth of field in this shot is approximately 5 feet in front of and behind Angela. The depth of field is not deep enough to include the leaves behind her. The "softness" provides a pleasing background.

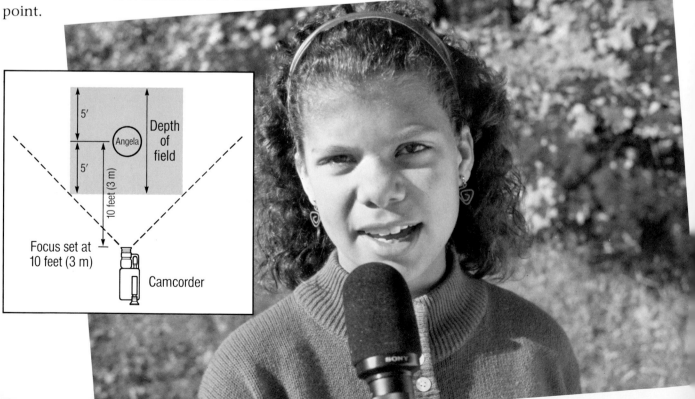

Auto Elimination

When we look quickly from one thing to another—say David on our left and Clara on our right—we first see one, then the other. Our brains usually skip over whatever is between them, such as Ms. Mason.

A camcorder doesn't do that. When it is moved, or **panned**, from one object to another, it focuses on everything in between as well. It doesn't de-emphasize objects we don't want to see.

If the camera is panned too quickly, the image will be blurry. Unless this is a desired effect, it can be very distracting.

The Bumps

When we walk, we bounce. If we walk over a bumpy surface, such as cobblestones, the bouncing effect can be jarring. Even so, our brains smooth out the bumps for us so that what we see in front of us doesn't seem to jump around.

As you pan, or move, the camcorder from the boy on the left to the girl on the right, it must pass by the woman in the middle. Although our eyes might not "see" the middle person, the camcorder will.

The camcorder, unfortunately, records every little bump. Even holding the camcorder in your hand will cause the picture to drift, or move slightly, because it's hard to hold the camera absolutely still. Tripods (three-legged stabilizing devices), unipods (a one-legged device), or even a wall or the ground make good picture stabilizers.

● ●

What we choose to put inside the frame, how we light it, and how we choose to move the camera or objects within the frame are what make a good video maker, not just a picture taker. It's like the difference between taking a photograph and a snapshot.

Three common camcorder formats are shown above: **1)** VHS; **2)** Hi8; and **3)** VHS-C. The size and shape of the different videotapes, shown at right, also vary.

Chapter Two

CHOOSING A CAMCORDER FORMAT

There are currently three basic camcorder formats—VHS, Beta, and 8mm—and variations within those formats. Camcorder format characteristics include the size and shape of the videotape cassette, the type of videotape, the way picture and sound are recorded onto the tape, and how the videotape is threaded around the record heads.

VHS has four variations: regular VHS, VHS-C (a compact version of VHS), S-VHS (an enhanced version of VHS), and S-VHS-C (compact and enhanced). There are also two types of 8mm— regular 8mm and Hi8—and two kinds of Beta, regular and ED (enhanced definition) Beta.

"Enhanced" means that manufacturers have worked to improve the picture quality with better color, brightness, and so on. The cost of enhanced formats is more expensive than that of standard formats. Yet another format, 4mm, is in development.

With the introduction of digital video (which is similar to digital audio, the technology used to record music on compact discs), and high definition television (HDTV), who knows how many more formats will be available in the future? In all, it's a dizzying range of choices!

Because of these format differences, VHS, Beta, and 8mm are not compatible, which means that videotapes recorded on one format cannot be played back on a different format videocassette recorder (VCR). For example, you cannot play Beta tapes on a VHS recorder. Some formats are more popular than others in certain parts of the country. Depending on where you live, camera accessories and prerecorded movies may not be available in all formats. So if you have a choice of formats, remember that buying a camcorder means making a commitment to a particular format.

As far as picture quality is concerned, none of the formats or brands of camcorder is necessarily better than any other. There are, however, considerable differences in the sound quality, size, and weight of camcorders, as well as convenience in shooting.

What to Look For

In judging picture quality, the criteria should include:
- clarity
- accuracy
- low-light recording ability

Clarity. Evaluate the camcorder's ability to record an image that is detailed, sharp, stable, undistorted, and in focus from edge to edge. The image should be free of "snow" or other kinds of picture static—called "noise."

The best way to check a camcorder's clarity is to shoot a brightly lit scene with the camcorder focused on a detailed object. Ask the camcorder salesperson to set up an "alignment chart" that shows multiple circles, lines, squares, and rectangles. If such a chart is not available, shoot a page from a telephone book or the classified ad section of a newspaper.

Play the scene back on a VCR. You may find that all camcorders exhibit some clarity problems. If so, choose the camcorder that does the best job.

You can test how clear a picture your camcorder records by shooting an alignment chart or another detailed object, such as a map.

When you buy videotape, you don't necessarily get more quality for more money. Although professional grade videotapes cost more than standard grade videotapes, to the human eye there is no difference in quality, according to a recent study.

Low-light recording ability. Realizing that most people who use camcorders will not bother with supplemental light, many manufacturers advertise their camcorder's ability to record in low light (remember that acceptable light to our eyes is "low light" to a camcorder). You may have seen advertisements that say a particular camcorder is rated at "7 lux" or a very low "2 lux."

Lux is a measurement used to indicate a camera's sensitivity to light. The more sensitive a camcorder is to light, the lower its lux rating. Bright sun is rated at about 100,000 lux. With current technology (which is always improving), a camcorder needs at least 500 to 800 lux to record a good quality image with accurate color. While a camcorder might be able to "see" something in only 2 to 10 lux, that does not mean the recorded image will be good. At such low light levels, the picture will likely be dim, shadowy, grainy, and off-color.

Accuracy. Evaluate the camcorder's ability to faithfully record color. You don't need expensive testing equipment; simply set up a scene with a person, a white object (such as a tablecloth), and a bowl of colorful fruit or similar prop. Record the image—both indoors and outdoors, if possible—and play it back on a VCR.

Are the skin tones true to life? If the person is wearing red (the most difficult color for a camcorder to reproduce), is the color "bleeding" onto other areas of the scene? Are the whites white, or do they have a green or red tint? Can you see a difference between similar shades of one color? If not, choose another camcorder. Again, you may have to buy the camcorder that is least objectionable.

Where to Buy a Camcorder

Thoroughly research the field to learn about the latest features and formats available *before* you buy a camcorder. The important features found on most camcorders are described in the next chapter. To do research, visit your local library. There you will find a variety of magazines aimed at video hobbyists. Often these magazines publish articles about every brand, model, and format of camcorder on the market, plus a host of accessories.

Another excellent source of information is *Consumer Reports* magazine, which rates and compares many consumer products. You can also ask your friends, teachers, and relatives who own camcorders what they like and don't like about their models. Finally, visit one or more electronics stores to see what's available in your area.

Often, daily newspapers and specialty magazines carry advertisements from direct-mail companies that sell name-brand equipment for less than most retail stores. But there are some risks and inconveniences that come with the cheaper prices. If your camcorder needs repairs, some direct-mail companies will not provide service, and some retail stores may not want to fix your camcorder if you did not buy it there.

While it is true that some camcorders are more sensitive to light than others—which means that they need less light to see an image—no camcorder will record good quality pictures in low light.

Some camcorder features you'll need to know about include 1) the pause button; 2) the view-finder; and 3) the zoom lens.

Chapter Three

CAMCORDER FEATURES

The camcorder works by letting light pass through the lens, which focuses the light to create an image. Inside a newer model camcorder, an electronic device called a charged coupling device (CCD), or "chip," translates the image from light energy into electronic energy. The electronic image is recorded and stored on videotape. When you play back the videotape, the VCR and television "read" the stored electronic energy and translate it back into images we can see. Many parts are needed to make that happen, of course, but to the average video buff it's the camcorder's operating features that are important.

Viewfinder

The viewfinder is what you look through to "frame" or compose the image. Almost all camcorders have an electronic viewfinder—a small black-and-white (or color) television picture. Some camcorders have an optical viewfinder, similar to a still camera's viewfinder. Electronic viewfinders are preferable, because they show you everything that is being recorded.

Lens

The lens is the camcorder's eye. It focuses light into an image that can be electronically recorded. The most popular—perhaps the only—lens you will find on a camcorder is a zoom lens. A zoom lens is many lenses in one. By pushing a switch or turning a small handle, you can adjust the focal length to widen or

This subject was shot at three ranges of the zoom lens:
1) wide-angle; **2)** the middle; and **3)** the telephoto.

narrow the lens's field of view. A zoom lens lets us get closer to or farther away from objects without moving either the camera or the subject of the picture.

The focal length of a zoom lens—the range between the widest and the tightest angles the lens can capture—is expressed as a ratio. Common ratios are 6:1 or 8:1. This means that the telephoto focal length of the lens is six or eight times greater than the widest angle focal length. Most camcorder zoom lenses offer very tight telephoto focal lengths, but wide-angle lengths that are not really very wide. You can increase the wide angle of the lens by buying a wide-angle adapter that fits onto the end of the zoom lens. The adapter allows you to create a variety of special effects.

Auto Iris

Adjusting the iris to allow more or less light to pass through the aperture to the lens is called "setting the exposure." Too much light will result in a picture that is overexposed, or too light (and it could also damage the delicate electronic parts in the camcorder). Too little light will result in a picture that is underexposed, or too dark.

Often you will want to shoot a scene that has a wide range of exposure. For example, you might move from outside, which is brightly lit by the sun, to inside, which may only have a few "practicals," or indoor lamps. Manually adjusting the iris to allow for the differences in exposure is difficult. Your picture may fluctuate from dark to light to "normal."

The iris opens and closes, letting in more or less light.

Scenes with a wide range of contrast between light and dark areas are difficult to capture accurately on video.

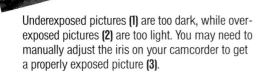

Underexposed pictures **(1)** are too dark, while over-exposed pictures **(2)** are too light. You may need to manually adjust the iris on your camcorder to get a properly exposed picture **(3)**.

Many camcorders have an "auto iris" feature that automatically adjusts the exposure to what the camera thinks is correct. Many scenes contain significant ranges of contrast between light and dark objects, however. Some scenes may be "back-lit"; that is, the sun or light source is behind the subject, making the background brighter than the subject itself. Or the subject may be in shadow. In these situations, the auto iris will be fooled. It will set the exposure for the brightly lit background, making the subject too dark.

Some camcorders offer a "backlit" feature. When turned on, it can override the auto iris slightly and increase the exposure on the subject, making it brighter. Because it is often imprecise, auto iris is a feature that you may want to avoid. If you have a choice, get a camcorder with a manual iris adjustment.

Focus

As discussed earlier, in order for the camcorder's lens to focus, or see an object clearly, you must set the focus ring to the required distance. All camcorders have an automatic focusing feature, called auto focus, which can focus the lens for you. There are two types of auto focus methods used on camcorders: *infrared triangulation* and *contrast maximization*.

Because many of the camcorder's automatic features have limitations, it is important to know how to override them and make manual adjustments.

Auto Focus

Infrared triangulation works by "shooting" an infrared beam of light at a target. The system measures how long it takes the beam to reflect back to the camcorder's sensor, translates that time into distance, and sets the focus. Problems can arise when the infrared light beam either gets absorbed by the target and doesn't reflect, or when the beam is shot away from the target that you want to be in focus.

Contrast maximization works by adjusting the focus of the lens until maximum contrast between light and dark is achieved—which occurs when the picture is in focus. With this system, it can be difficult to shoot objects with busy or repeating patterns, such as herringbone suits. Because of these limitations, both systems will often search or "hunt" for focus. This annoying shifting in and out of focus happens most when shooting at low light levels, because of the shallow depth of field—or when panning across objects that are at different distances from the camcorder.

Point at which camcorder is focused

Camcorder's field of view

Line of dancers will be out of focus

Infrared beam of light

Camcorder

White Balance

Our world is filled with different kinds of light: the sun; incandescent light (used in many home lighting fixtures); fluorescent; tungsten; sodium vapor (often used in street lights); and more. Each of these light sources emits a different color of light—that's right, different colors.

Light, like sound, is a kind of energy. Light energy is composed of waves of different lengths. These waves are part of the electromagnetic spectrum, which also includes x-rays, gamma rays, radio waves, and microwaves. Visible light—the part of the spectrum we can see—is just a small part of the spectrum. If you've ever seen a prism, you know that it breaks down light into different colors, from blue and purple on one end of the visible light spectrum to red and orange on the other. When all the colors of the spectrum are combined, however, we see them as white.

All light sources give off light energy of a certain color. Incandescent light from lamps is orange. Sodium vapor light is brownish, and fluorescent light can be green, blue, or yellow.

Different sources of light are often found together. In a home, for example, sunlight may stream through the kitchen window, while above the kitchen table there may be an incandescent light, and over the stove there may be a fluorescent fixture. Our brains compensate for different lighting sources by making everything we see look "normal." White looks white, blue looks blue, and red looks red—even though the light source might be a green fluorescent light, a brownish sodium vapor light, or a mixture of the two.

Camcorders are not so smart. To record an image with colors that look "normal," they must be adjusted according to the type of light falling on a subject. **White balance** is the term used to describe the electronic circuitry in a camcorder that ensures that colors look normal under various lighting conditions. With the flip of a switch, the camcorder will automatically set the white balance.

As with all automated features, however, the white balance circuit can be tricked into making poor quality pictures, especially if the scene contains mostly one color. That's why most camcorders provide manually operated white balance settings for sunlight or incandescent lighting. Some camcorders also have a setting for fluorescent lighting.

Shutter Speed

The **shutter** is a mechanical or electronic device that controls the amount of time a frame of film or videotape is exposed to light. In video, the normal **shutter speed** is $1/30$th of a second, which means that 30 frames are exposed each second. This may seem like a short amount of time, but it isn't. A lot of movement can occur in $1/30$th of a second—especially when shooting events such as a tennis match or a bike race. If you "freeze frame," or stop the image during playback, you'll see how blurry it is. The blurriness is caused by the movement of the subject within the frame.

Some camcorders have shutter settings that can be used to shoot fast-moving objects. Using a high-speed shutter setting, such as $1/800$th of a second, will eliminate blurring images. In most cases, blurring presents a problem only when you want to freeze or stop fast action.

To properly expose a picture using a high-speed shutter setting, you need bright light, preferably sunlight. The high-speed shutter setting used in dim light will result in a dark, off-color picture. That's because the shutter opens for such a short time.

To get a picture of fast action that isn't blurry, you may need to use a shutter speed of up to 1/800th of a second—or faster.

Sound

Sound recording is not one of a camcorder's strengths. Even though tests suggest that the Beta and Hi8 formats produce better sound than the VHS format, the built-in microphone on all camcorders severely limits sound quality. The mike is designed to record speech rather than music. Using a remote rather than the built-in microphone will improve the sound quality of your videos.

All camcorders automatically control the **gain**, or sound level, of what is being recorded. This feature is included so that you do not have to manually adjust the volume as it changes. However, this automatic feature can be fooled, too.

When someone is speaking close to the microphone, the gain control will automatically set the recording level so that the voice will be recorded clearly. But when someone speaks far away from the microphone, or speaks softly, the auto gain control will turn up the gain to "hear" the person better. When the gain control is turned up, the microphone also begins to "hear" background sounds, such as the noise of the camcorder's motors and gears or people talking in the background.

Review/Playback

All camcorders double as VCRs. The "review" feature allows you to review the last few seconds of what you've recorded, using the viewfinder as a TV. Some camcorders have a built-in speaker through which you can hear the sound as the tape is played back.

When connected to another VCR, the playback feature also permits you to dub, or make copies of, videotapes. This can come in handy when you want to edit the videotapes you've shot by putting in new scenes or shortening existing scenes.

Special Effects

Many camcorders let you create special effects, such as time-lapse photography, stop action, fading to and from black, and titles.

Some camcorder models have a character generator that allows you to superimpose titles over a scene as you shoot it. On some models, you can even choose what color to make the titles.

All camcorders have a "stationary erase head," which is activated when you push the record button. The erase head electronically cleans the videotape of old information (picture, sound, or both, depending on the camcorder model) before recording something new. If the picture is erased, however, the stationary erase head creates a noticeable "glitch" or jump in the picture when it is turned on.

Some camcorders have a special editing feature called a "flying erase head." It allows you to make seamless edits, without glitches, when you press the pause button. This feature is not found on all camcorders. If you have a choice, buy a camcorder with a flying erase head.

The camcorder's character generator lets you create titles for your video.

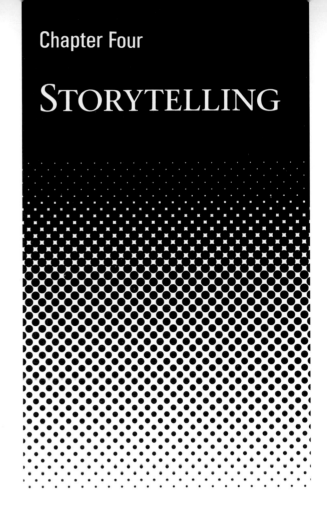

Chapter Four

STORYTELLING

Which came first: the music or the lyrics? The pictures or the words? It's an interesting question; one that different artists will answer differently. In the end, it really doesn't matter. What *does* matter is that the music and the lyrics, or the pictures and the words, work together to tell a story.

Every video must start with an idea for a story you want to share with an audience. The story could be as simple as documenting your younger brother's birthday party or as complex as shooting a spoof of *Indiana Jones*.

Elements of Storytelling

All good stories have three things in common: a beginning, a middle, and an end. The beginning of a story introduces the characters (real or imagined) and the locale (where the story takes place) and sets the stage for the action. The middle of the story develops the relationship between the characters, advances the action, and sets the stage for the outcome of the story. The end of the story concludes the action.

It sounds simple enough. But when you've got an idea for a story, at first all the elements are rolling around inside your head. Often, specific ideas and scenes will come as a flash of creative energy—and depart just as quickly.

Write it down. The best way to begin your video is to write down your story on paper. Explain the idea to yourself and others who read it. Start with a synopsis, or summary, of the story idea. Then expand the idea into its three main components: beginning, middle, and end.

If you think of your story as "soup," put it

aside for a while and let it "cook" in your head. As with any good soup, your story will benefit from adding "a little of this or a little of that." In other words, change, add, rearrange, or remove parts of your story after reading it and discussing it with others.

Drama or documentary? Basically, there are two kinds of stories you can choose to tell: a drama, in which the story and the characters are imaginary, or a documentary, in which the story and the characters are real. No matter which kind of story you choose to tell, remember that all storytellers have a point of view, or an opinion, about the story, the characters, and the outcome. There is no such thing as an objective documentary. What you choose to show with the camera—and what you choose *not* to show—establishes your point of view.

A drama is a made-up story (it may be based on a true incident, but it is still fiction) that uses real people (actors) pretending to be imaginary characters. What you as the videomaker are asking the audience to do is accept the imaginary story even though it is presented on a TV screen by actors. You are asking the audience to "suspend its disbelief." Your job, like Shakespeare's and Spielberg's before you, is to get the audience to accept the story and project themselves into it.

A documentary is just that: a document or record of an event, such as a battle, the birth of a chick, a parade, or a party. Unlike a drama, a documented event is not staged or planned; it happens, and you are there to record or document it. Nevertheless, you have choices to make, and those choices will result in a point of view or opinion about the event.

Whether you choose to make a drama or a documentary, when preparing your synopsis, be as visually descriptive as you can. Use words that translate into images in your mind. For example, here are two descriptive passages from a script for a drama. Which do you think better describes what the video writer wanted us to see?

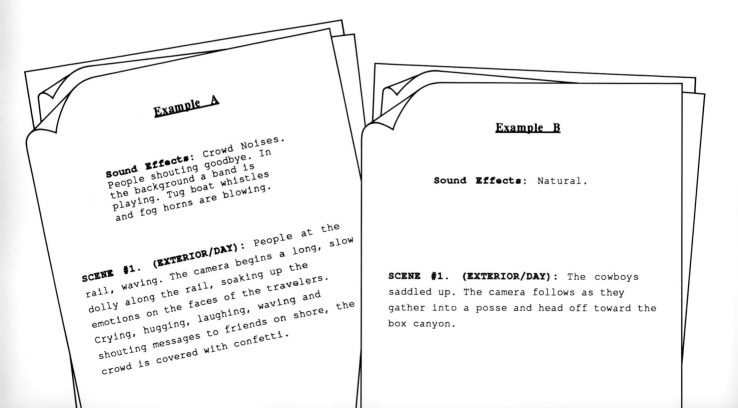

Example A

Sound Effects: Crowd Noises. People shouting goodbye. In the background a band is playing. Tug boat whistles and fog horns are blowing.

SCENE #1. (EXTERIOR/DAY): People at the rail, waving. The camera begins a long, slow dolly along the rail, soaking up the emotions on the faces of the travelers. Crying, hugging, laughing, waving and shouting messages to friends on shore, the crowd is covered with confetti.

Example B

Sound Effects: Natural.

SCENE #1. (EXTERIOR/DAY): The cowboys saddled up. The camera follows as they gather into a posse and head off toward the box canyon.

The Shooting Script

The shooting script is the "blueprint" of your video. It describes in video terms the action, scenes, and dialogue to be shot. The script is prepared from the synopsis and is used to make sure that all the elements of the story are covered—that nothing is forgotten. Reviewing your synopsis will help you "see" the scenes you'll need to shoot to tell your story.

The example below shows a common kind of shooting script. Your script does not have to be this formal, but using a consistent format to lay out the scene descriptions and dialogue will help you, the crew, and the actors when it comes time to shoot.

•••••••••••••••••••••••• Format of a Shooting Script ••••••••••••••••••••••••

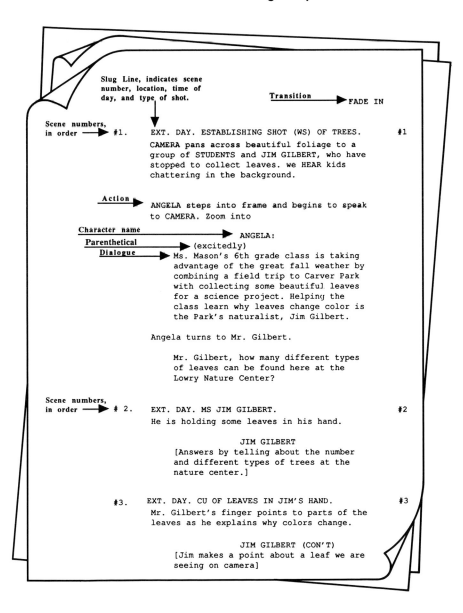

Slug Line, indicates scene number, location, time of day, and type of shot.

Transition ▶ FADE IN

Scene numbers, in order ▶ #1.   EXT. DAY. ESTABLISHING SHOT (WS) OF TREES.   #1
CAMERA pans across beautiful foliage to a group of STUDENTS and JIM GILBERT, who have stopped to collect leaves. we HEAR kids chattering in the background.

Action ▶ ANGELA steps into frame and begins to speak to CAMERA. Zoom into

Character name ▶ ANGELA:
Parenthetical ▶ (excitedly)
Dialogue ▶ Ms. Mason's 6th grade class is taking advantage of the great fall weather by combining a field trip to Carver Park with collecting some beautiful leaves for a science project. Helping the class learn why leaves change color is the Park's naturalist, Jim Gilbert.

Angela turns to Mr. Gilbert.

Mr. Gilbert, how many different types of leaves can be found here at the Lowry Nature Center?

Scene numbers, in order ▶ # 2.   EXT. DAY. MS JIM GILBERT.   #2
He is holding some leaves in his hand.

JIM GILBERT
[Answers by telling about the number and different types of trees at the nature center.]

#3.   EXT. DAY. CU OF LEAVES IN JIM'S HAND.   #3
Mr. Gilbert's finger points to parts of the leaves as he explains why colors change.

JIM GILBERT (CON'T)
[Jim makes a point about a leaf we are seeing on camera]

Here is how a script looks for a video called "Field Trip to Carver Park," a news report prepared by students in a media instruction class. The report is for "Totally Radical TV," a student-produced show that is seen on the school's closed-circuit television system. The kids in the media class take turns doing the various jobs of camera operator, production assistant, reporter, and so forth.

For this report, Angela and Steve are the reporters. Their assignment is to take a crew to Carver Park to show the fall colors and to interview students who are collecting leaves for a science project and the naturalist who is guiding them.

Totally Radical TV

News Script

Title:	6th Grade Field Trip to Carver Park
Length:	3:00
Location:	Carver Park Nature Center
Teacher:	Ms. Mason
Production Date:	October 15
Air Date:	October 19
Camera Operator:	Jenny Uglem
Assistant:	David Olson
Reporters:	Angela Conklin
	Steve Braun

FADE IN

#1.   EXT. DAY. ESTABLISHING SHOT (WS) OF TREES.   #1
        Camera pans across beautiful foliage to where a group of STUDENTS and
        GILBERT, a naturalist, have stopped to collect leaves.

            SFX: Kids chattering about leaves. Mr. Gilbert
            is explaining how leaves change color.

        ANGELA steps into frame and begins to speak to CAMERA. Zoom into MS.

                        ANGELA:
            Ms. Mason's 6th grade class is taking
            advantage of the great fall weather by
            combining a field trip to Carver Park
            with collecting some beautiful leaves for
            a science project. Helping the class
            learn why leaves change color is the
            Park's naturalist, Jim Gilbert.

        Angela turns to Mr. Gilbert.

            Mr. Gilbert, how many different types of
            leaves can be found here at the Lowry
            Nature Center?

#2.   EXT. DAY. MS JIM GILBERT.
            He is holding some leaves in his hand.   #2

                        JIM GILBERT
            [Answers by telling about the number and
            different types of trees at the nature
            center.]

#3.   EXT. DAY. CU OF LEAVES IN JIM GILBERT'S HAND.
        Mr. Gilbert's finger points to parts of the leaves as he explains why   #3
        colors change.

                    JIM GILBERT (CON'T)
            [Jim makes a point about a leaf we are
            seeing on camera]

#4.   EXT. DAY. CU OF ANGELA.
        Angela reacts to Jim's explanation, then asks a second question.   #4

                        ANGELA
            Do leaves make food for their trees?

#5.   EXT. DAY. OVER THE SHOULDER 2-SHOT OF ANGELA AND JIM.   #5
        Jim answers the question.

                        JIM GILBERT
                  [Answers question]

        Angela thanks Jim and turns toward camera. Zoom into MS of Angela.

                        ANGELA
                  Thanks, Mr. Gilbert. Now, to find out
                  what the kids have learned during their
                  field trip today, here's Steve…

                                        CUT TO:

#6.   EXT. DAY. STEVE IS SURROUNDED BY SEVERAL KIDS.   #6
        STEVE asks a question, then passes the mike to get each kid's answer.

                        STEVE
                  Jenny, what's the most important thing
                  you've learned here at Carver Park today?

        The camera zooms into JENNY. Then pans to each kid as he/she responds.

                        JENNY
                  [Jenny's answer]

#7.   EXT. DAY. CU STEVE.
        Kids and Mr. Gilbert continue to examine leaves.   #7

                        STEVE
                  Earlier today, Mr. Gilbert showed the
                  kids one of the special birds taken care
                  of at the park. Here with the story on
                  how a wounded Kestral Hawk was nursed
                  back to health, is Angela.

                                        CUT TO:

#8.   INT. DAY. WS MR. GILBERT, HAWK AND KIDS AT TABLE.   #8
        Mr. Gilbert is telling the kids about the one-winged Kestral Hawk.

                        JIM GILBERT
               [Telling Hawk story to the kids.]
                                                                    #9

#9.   INT. DAY. JIM'S POV OF KIDS LOOKING AT HIM.
        One of the kids interjects a question.

                           KID
               [Question to Jim Gilbert.]
                                                                    #10

#10.   INT. DAY. CU JIM GILBERT.
        Jim holds the Hawk as he answers the question.

                        JIM GILBERT
               [Jim asks the kids to notice its only
        wing.]
                                                                    #11

#11.   INT. DAY. REACTION SHOT OF KID.
        Kids are surprised to learn the bird has only one wing.

                           KID   CUT TO:
               [Response.]

#12.   EXT. DAY. 2-SHOT OF ANGELA AND STEVE SURROUNDED BY KIDS.   #12
        As Angela and Steve wrap-up the story, the kids start tossing leaves a
        them.

                        ANGELA & STEVE
               [Ad lib reaction to one-winged Hawk.]
        That's our report from Carver Park. It
        seems like these kids are done learning
        for today [they react to leaves being
        tossed at them], so we'll turn it back to
        the studio. This is Steve Braun and
        Angela Conklin reporting.

                                              FADE OUT

Storyboards

After you've written the script, you may find it helpful to visualize the script by drawing pictures of the important scenes. These pictures are called **storyboards**. They can be anything from a rough sketch that shows the flow of action to elaborate renderings or still photographs, precise in every detail.

Storyboards can be useful in anticipating production problems and making clear to the crew and actors what you, the videomaker, want. Below is a simple storyboard of four of the scenes taken from the "Field Trip to Carver Park" script.

Notice that the scene number and description—called "copy"—plus the dialogue—called "speeches"—are written below each storyboard picture.

Now that you know what you're going to do, it's time to determine how you're going to do it.

STORYBOARD

TOTALLY RADICAL TV

TITLE: 6th GRADE FIELD TRIP TO CARVER PARK

LENGTH: 3:00

LOCATION: CARVER PARK NATURE CENTER

TEACHER: MS. MASON

PRODUCTION DATE: OCTOBER 15

AIR DATE: OCTOBER 19

CAMERA OPERATOR: JENNY UGLEM

ASSISTANT: DAVID OLSON

REPORTERS: ANGELA CONKLIN STEVE BRAUN

SCENE 1: WS PAN OF TREES. CAMERA FINDS GROUP OF KIDS. ANGELA STEPS INTO FRAME.

SCENE 2: MS JIM GILBERT HOLDING LEAVES IN HIS HAND.

SCENE 3: CU OF LEAVES IN JIM'S HAND. JIM POINTS TO PARTS OF LEAVES.

SCENE 4: CU OF ANGELA. ANGELA REACTS TO JIM'S EXPLANATION.

Chapter Five

THE GRAMMAR OF VIDEO

Video, like film, is a language—a visual language, rather than a spoken language. Video and film have a grammar of their own. It is as important to know the grammatical structure of video to tell your story in pictures as it is to know the grammatical structure of English to tell your story in writing.

Although grammatical rules can be broken, they provide a common ground of under-standing that helps to communicate your idea to others. After all, you want the audience to understand what's happening.

Here is a simple grammar of video:

A *shot* is similar to a sentence.

A *sequence* is similar to a paragraph.

A *segment* is similar to a chapter.

Cuts, *fades*, and *dissolves* are transitions that help advance the story visually.

The Types of Shots

There are three basic types of shots:
1) an *establishing shot* (or *wide shot*), abbreviated as "ES" or "WS"
2) a *medium shot*, abbreviated as "MS"
3) a *close-up*, abbreviated as "CU"

An *establishing shot* identifies the location, introduces the characters, and defines the relationship between the characters and the location. Scene 1 from "Field Trip to Carver Park" is such a shot.

A *medium shot* advances the action. It gives us the next bit of information we need to understand why the kids are in the park.

A *close-up* reveals the details of emotion and personality. Scene 3 of "Field Trip to Carver Park" is such a shot.

An establishing shot (1) shows the kids at Carver Park. The medium shot (2) zooms in to Angie's upper body. A close-up (3) shows the leaf in Jim Gilbert's hand.

There are many other types of shots, including *reverse angle* (abbreviated as "RA"), *point-of-view* (POV), *reaction shot*, *extreme close-up* (ECU), and *extreme wide angle* (EWA).

A *reverse angle* is a shot taken from the opposite angle of the previous shot. The name reverse angle implies that another shot from the opposite angle will be taken. If no additional shot is planned, the shot is referred to as an *over-the-shoulder* shot, abbreviated as "OS."

A *point-of-view* shot is taken from the subject's point of view—the camera looks at what the subject sees. Scene 9 of "Field Trip to Carver Park" is such a shot. We could stay on Scene 8 of Jim Gilbert and the bird at the table, but looking at the kids from Jim's perspective helps the audience become involved with the characters and shows that the kids are paying attention to what Jim Gilbert is saying.

A *reaction shot* is a medium or close-up view of the subject reacting to what he or she has just seen, felt, or heard. Scene 11 of "Field Trip to Carver Park" is a reaction shot, because after Scene 10 we cut back to Clara's face to watch her reaction to the question.

An *extreme close-up* and an *extreme wide-angle* are just what their names imply —very close or very wide views of a scene. If we chose to, we could shoot an ex- treme close-up of the bird's head. Because the head would fill the entire frame, the shot would be an extreme close-up.

Keep in mind that these terms are relative. A shot of the bird's head is an extreme close-up because we show only parts of

This reverse angle shot was taken from the opposite angle as the medium shot on the facing page.

The reaction shot **(above)** shows Clara's reaction to what Jim Gilbert is saying. The extreme close-up, **(left)** shows the bird's head.

Shooting a
high-angle shot

A high-angle shot

Shooting a low-angle shot

its body. But a shot of a whole ant could be called a wide-angle shot.

By varying the shots—going from a wide shot to a medium shot, then to a close-up and back to another medium shot—we give variety to the story and tell it in an interesting and meaningful way. Vary the shots in your video not just for the sake of change, but to advance the story and maintain interest.

Changing Angles

Changing the angle of a shot changes the mood of a scene and is a tool you can use to help tell your story. Angle changes can also add drama, a new dimension, or a fresh

viewpoint. Here are a few common angles you should know.

High-angle shot. Shooting the subject from above makes the subject appear smaller or dependent.

Low-angle shot. Shooting the subject from below makes the subject appear larger and commanding.

An eye-level shot

Shooting an
eye-level shot

A low-angle shot

Eye-level shot. By placing the camera at eye level, we treat the subject as an equal—neither dependent nor dominating. It's always best to shoot people at eye level, unless you want to create a certain mood by using a high- or low-angle shot. It's more enjoyable to watch children and pets photographed at their level.

Of course, moving things are always changing position. When making a video, we often have to compromise. If the scene starts with the subject seated and ends with the subject standing, where should we place the camera? Midway between a seated and standing height would be one solution, but not necessarily the best. Keeping the camera height at a standing position is another solution. We often stand next to a person seated at a table. It's natural for us to look down at someone who is sitting.

Jump Cut

A **jump cut** isn't one shot, but two similar shots (say medium shots) of the same person or action with the subject in a slightly different position in each shot. The "jump" occurs when the two shots are edited together and the subject appears to abruptly move or "jump" from one part of the screen to another. Jump cuts can be avoided by placing a different kind of shot (say a reverse angle or a close-up) between the two medium shots.

Transitional Shots

Transitional shots are used to visually take us from one part of the story to the next, or from one location to the next. They help the audience follow time or location changes. There are many transitional shots, including *fade-in/out shots*, *zoom shots*, and *rack-focus shots*.

A *fade-in* is a shot that begins in black and slowly gets brighter as the iris is opened, allowing more light to pass through the lens. Fade-ins are done by using the manual iris

control on the lens or using the "auto fade" feature on many camcorders. A fade-in is most often used at the beginning of a sequence. A *fade-out* begins as a bright scene and slowly gets darker as the iris is closed. A fade-out is most often used at the end of a sequence.

Zooming the lens to change the angle of view can be a way to make a transition from one part of the story to another. Zooming in from a wide shot to a close-up—or the reverse—is a powerful way to focus the viewer's attention.

In video language, "rack" means to change. When we "rack focus," we focus first on one object, then another, to reveal a relationship between the two. For example, if we wanted to show the relationship between the signpost on the path and the people at Carver Park walking in the woods, we could first focus tightly on the sign. Then, as the students walked into the frame, we could rack focus from the sign to the kids. Because this transitional shot draws attention to itself, it should be used sparingly.

This sequence of rack-focus shots shows how a relationship is revealed between the sign at the park and the group of students.

Pan Shot

Another way to reveal information and maintain the audience's interest is to pan, or move the camera horizontally. (Vertical movements of the camera are called **tilts**.) Pan shots can also show the relationship between objects. The beginning of Scene 1 of "Field Trip to Carver Park" is a pan shot of the trees. As the camera moves from the trees to the students, a relationship between them is established.

A **swish pan** is a fast-moving pan that creates an intentionally blurry image. It is used as a transition between two scenes. For a swish pan to be effective, the end of Scene A and the beginning of Scene B must be "swishing." The **cut**, or change, from Scene A to Scene B occurs in the middle of a swish.

Pan shots are also used to follow moving action, such as someone walking down the street or a race car going around a track. The camera moves to follow the action, but the camera operator stays in one place.

SWISH PAN

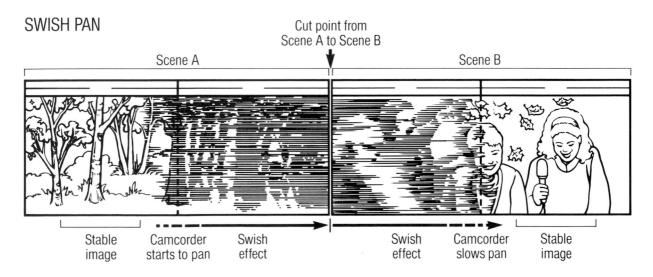

Cut point from Scene A to Scene B

Scene A

Scene B

Stable image | Camcorder starts to pan | Swish effect

Swish effect | Camcorder slows pan | Stable image

One way to stabilize the camcorder is to use a unipod.

Camera Stabilizers

Most film and videomakers do not want the audience to be aware of the camera or its movement. They call it "being transparent." Their goal is to shoot smooth, steady shots that don't bounce, twist, or turn. Using a dolly is one way to stabilize the camera. Tripods and unipods do the same job. A tripod, as you recall, is a three-legged platform with adjustable legs that allows you to change the camera's height.

Dolly/Tracking Shots

Another way to follow a subject is to **dolly** or **track** by moving the camcorder along with the subject. A dolly shot moves in and out with the subject, while a tracking shot travels parallel to the subject. Technically, a dolly is a wheeled platform that holds the camera and camera operator. On professional shoots, the dolly is pushed or pulled by a *dolly pusher.*

If you don't have access to an automobile, you can use a wagon for a dolly.

You can create dolly or tracking shots by using any wheeled device: a wagon, skateboard, wheelchair, or automobile (preferably a station wagon). Remember, though, that each time you go over a crack in a sidewalk or a bump in the road, the dolly will bounce, and so will the camcorder.

Use an automobile as a camera dolly only with adult supervision.

42

Handheld Shots

Handheld shots are those that you shoot without using a dolly, tripod, or unipod. Handheld shots can be very shaky or wobbly, so it's important to brace yourself and hold the camcorder as firmly as you can.

Here are a few tips for getting steady handheld shots:

- Flex your knees. Your legs act like shock absorbers. If you lock your knees, your legs won't absorb the bumps.
- Lean against a wall, fence, tree, or other object—even another person. This will take the weight off your legs and leave you free to concentrate on the shot.
- When using your body as a dolly, you can maintain a steady shot by keeping the camcorder slightly off your shoulder. This way, you'll minimize the bounce as you walk.

When taking handheld shots, try to lean against something—even another person will work.

Chapter Six

COMPOSING PICTURES

Composing pictures is the art of arranging objects within the camera's frame and establishing a relationship between the camera and those objects. Good composition is an art that requires creativity and an understanding of some fundamental rules. Here are explanations of some of the basics that you will want to know about.

Aspect Ratio

The shape of a television picture is rectangular. The size relationship between the height and the width of a rectangle is referred to as its **aspect ratio**. A television picture is a horizontal rectangle with an aspect ratio of 3:4—that is, 3 units high by 4 units wide.

Every part of the camcorder/television system has the same aspect ratio: the viewfinder, the camcorder, and the television screen. You can turn the camcorder on its side to make a vertical rather than horizontal composition, but the image you record will also be sideways. (This is different than a still film camera, which can take vertical pictures.)

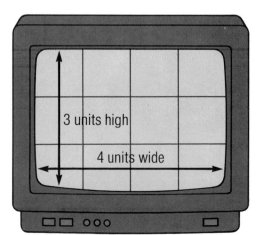

3 units high
4 units wide

The Rule of Three

Life is full of rules, most of which tend to make things difficult. The "rule of three," however, makes the task of composing images easy! The rule applies to all rectangular compositions and helps you determine where to place an object within the frame. You can use the rule for moving or static objects, people, the horizon, and landscapes.

The rule of three divides the horizontal frame into three equal vertical and horizontal parts, creating nine smaller rectangles inside the frame. The rule states that if you place the subject on one of the imaginary lines, it will appear more dynamic than if the subject is placed between the lines. The object is said to be in the "upper third" or the "lower third" of the frame.

When you shoot two people talking to each other, make sure to include some lead space in front of each person. This lets the viewer know that the other person is offscreen.

Composing for People

Unless a person is looking directly at the camera, centering someone in the frame is not as interesting as placing her or him off to the side. If two people are talking to each other, and you shoot each one separately, the camera should "lead" the person—provide more space in front of the first person in the direction of the other person. This suggests to the viewer that the other person is there, just out of range of the camera's frame.

Displacing What Is There

Videography is a two-dimensional medium. There is height and width, but no depth (unless we're looking at a special 3-D video or film process). Depth is an illusion that we must create by lighting and by separating objects within the frame.

When we're talking about depth, we divide the frame into three basic areas: the foreground, middle ground, and background. Some background objects do not move. Trees, telephone poles, utility wires, lamps, and other household objects are good examples. If you compose a frame in which a person stands directly in front of one of these objects, it might look as though the object is growing out of his or her head.

This can be distracting to viewers, because the camera does not distinguish between objects in the foreground and objects in the background. If the objects are evenly lit and take up about the same amount of space in the frame, the camera will treat them equally. The result is that the background object blends into the foreground.

You can avoid this by controlling the lighting on the objects within the frame or by moving the foreground subject, the camera, or both to displace the offending object. Keeping the camcorder's lens set toward the wide-angle end of the zoom will help, too. The greater the telephoto setting, the more the lens will compress the foreground, middle ground, and background together.

Colors can also blend elements in a frame. A person dressed in a green suit tends to blend into a green hedge or a green lawn in the background. Choose your background with care. If you can, do what the professionals do: have a "wardrobe session" for the actors to bring clothes that are appropriate to the scene. You select the outfits you want them to wear. The wardrobe session will also assure that two actors in the same scene do not wear clothes that clash.

Screen Direction

To advance your story without confusing the audience about where people are, where they have been, or where they are going, you must establish—then maintain—**screen direction**. Screen direction orients the audience to the relationship of objects within a sequence. (Don't confuse screen direction with *continuity*, a term used to describe consistency between shots in a sequence. If a person is wearing a hat in one shot, and in the next shot the hat is missing, the scene lacks continuity.)

In the example to the right, Scene 1 shows a girl and a boy facing one another. In the following scenes, the director photographs them in such a way that they appear to be facing each other in a consistent and logical direction. In Scene 2, a medium shot of the boy, we know the girl is off-screen to the left—even though we can't see her—because the boy is looking in that direction. In Scene 3,

a medium shot of the girl, we know the boy is off-screen to the right, because the girl is looking in that direction.

1) A wide shot establishes a directional relationship between the two people. In other words, the girl is on the left looking to the right, and the boy is on the right looking to the left.
2) A medium shot of the boy maintains the proper screen direction by showing him looking to the left.
3) A medium shot of the girl shows her looking to the right.

Screen direction must also be maintained when you're moving from location to location. When people have to move from one location to another, let them walk *out* of the first scene and *into* the second. If people or objects leave one scene from the right side of the frame, they should enter the next scene from the left side of the frame. If you shoot a person heading toward the right side of the frame, make sure the person keeps going in the same direction in the next scene.

It may not always be possible to position the camcorder or the actors in a way that maintains screen direction. In fact, you should expect that it will not be possible to get every shot of a sequence in the proper screen direction. What to do?

Be prepared to shoot several *neutral shots*. A neutral shot is one in which the actors are photographed either coming toward the camera or going away from it. A neutral shot can be "sandwiched" between right or left directional shots to get rid of any discrepancy in screen direction.

When you shoot people entering or exiting the frame, make sure they are going the same direction, such as left to right.

Crossing the Imaginary Line

The best way to understand screen direction and to set up your camcorder so that you maintain correct screen direction is to draw an imaginary line between the camcorder and the actors—and never cross it.

In the example below, the camcorder is positioned so that player "A" is on *camera left* and player "B" is on *camera right*. The imaginary line has been drawn down the center of the playing court. As long as the camcorder stays in the patterned area below the imaginary line, the screen direction of the two players will remain consistent. If the camcorder crosses the line, it will appear that the players are jumping from one side of the court to the other each time you cut to a new shot.

Scale, Frames, and Point of View

Try to compose your shots so that the audience can see the size relationship between objects in the frame. For example, Scene 11 from "Field Trip to Carver Park" shows the hawk in relation to Clara, and the difference in size is very apparent.

When possible, compose your frame with an arch, windows, or trees on the outside edge, creating a frame within a frame.

If you show a person looking at something, the next shot should show what she is looking at—her point of view. The third shot could be the person's reaction to what she has just seen.

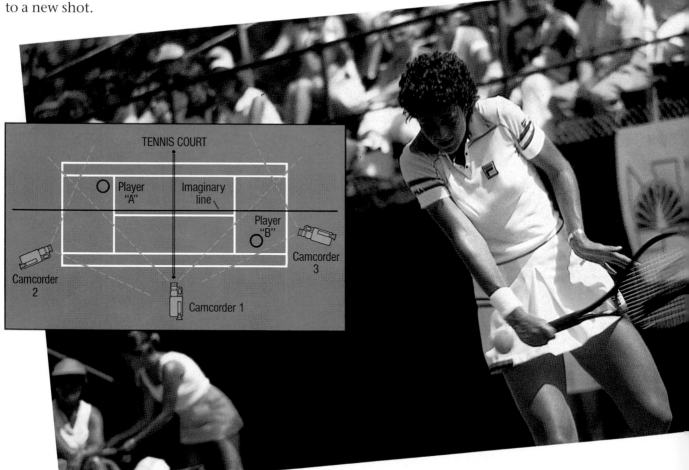

Chapter Seven

LIGHTING AND SOUND

Painters paint with color. Film and video-makers paint with light. Light—and shadow—give depth to the two-dimensional medium of videography. Light helps define the subject matter and create a mood. Lighting is an art that takes skill and patience to master.

Unless you have access to many lights, light stands, extension cords, and enough electrical power to turn them all on at once, don't worry too much about interior lighting. A small lighting kit will suffice for most scenes you will want to shoot.

. . . .

Electricity can be dangerous. An adult should supervise all interior lighting situations.

Even if you use just a few lights, there are a few tips you can learn that will help you achieve a good quality image.

First Things First

Always consider the *quality* of the light first, the *quantity* of the light second, and the iris adjustments on the camcorder last. Remember, light is used to give shape, texture, and mood to a two-dimensional scene. The quality of light you need to create the desired effect depends on your project. For example, let's say your video is a history of your family. The sequence you're working on now involves your grandfather telling stories of his childhood. Granddad is rather old and has an interesting face, with many "experience lines." You want to capture on video all the wonderful things age has written on his face. That decision tells you how to light the scene—with light that falls on Granddad's face in a way that highlights the wrinkles.

Interior Lighting Tips

Most static (nonmoving) lighting setups use three lights, each with a different purpose: a *key* light, which provides the primary (brightest) source of light; a *fill* light, which adds more light (filling in) to the area not lit by the key light; and the *back* light, which helps to separate the foreground subject from the background. Here is a typical three-light setup.

A typical three-light setup is shown below.

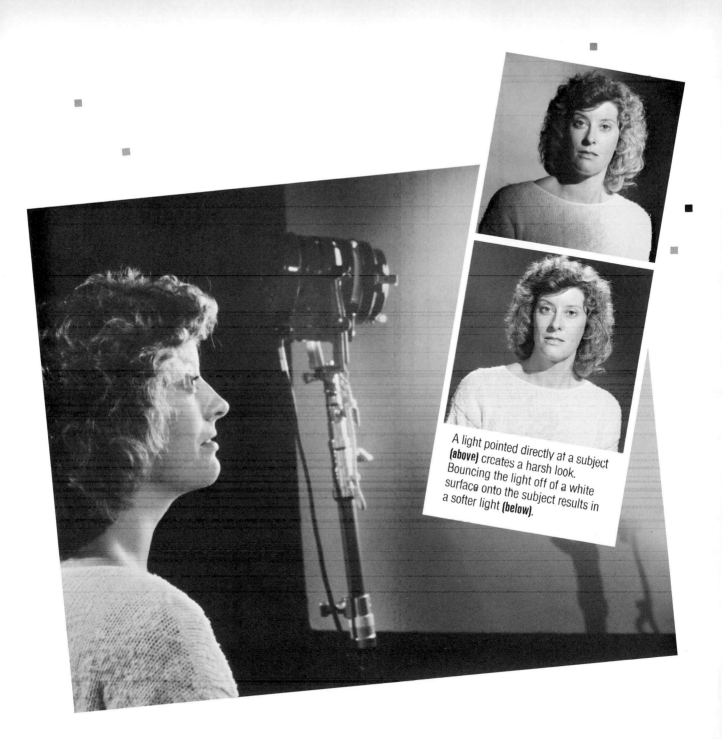

A light pointed directly at a subject **(above)** creates a harsh look. Bouncing the light off of a white surface onto the subject results in a softer light **(below).**

Pointing a light directly at a subject creates a harsh look. Unless that's the effect you want, soften the light by "bouncing," or reflecting, it off a white card (called a "bounce card"), the ceiling, or a wall.

Videos, of course, are not always static. The subject matter moves within the frame and the camera moves around a scene. A three-light setup works well for a static shot, but it may not work in a scene that covers a large area, or one in which the subject and/or camera will be moving, the entire scene must be lit evenly *and* the lights must be hidden from the camera's view.

Exterior Lighting Tips

The sun is the biggest light source of all. While the full sun provides a lot of light, it can sometimes work against us or play havoc with the camcorder's ability to handle light.

As a basic rule, try to shoot all of a scene either in sunlight or in shade. The adjustment between sunlight and shade is usually too great for even the most sophisticated camcorder's auto iris to make smoothly without making the viewer aware of the change. Manual adjustments may not be much better.

Most of the time it is best to keep your subject frontlit or sidelit, although there may be times when you would want to have the subject backlit.

Backlighting should only be used when you want to create a special effect, such as a mysterious mood. Frontlighting can often be harsh, and it's difficult to get people to look toward the sun without squinting. Sidelighting is generally considered ideal.

Sidelighting uses the sun as a key light. But often the shadow side of the person's face is too dark. That problem can be fixed with a bounce card, a 2 x 3 foot (.6 x .9 m) piece of white cardboard that is used as a "fill light" to bounce or reflect sunlight onto the shadow side of the subject. Look what happens when you add a bounce card to fill in the shadows.

Quantity of Light

After you've done the basic lighting setup, it's time to evaluate the quantity of light falling on the scene. No matter how artistic your lighting effect is, if the camcorder can't "see" it because it's too bright or too dark, you've done a lot of work for nothing.

The quantity of light needed is determined by how much light your camcorder needs to record a properly exposed image. Remember, your eye is *not* a good judge of the quantity

Outdoors, a subject may be 1) sidelit, 2) frontlit, or 3) backlit. Using a bounce card (right) creates a softer look.

of light needed by the camcorder. Black-and-white electronic viewfinders cannot distinguish contrast very well, and color viewfinders might not have color and tint controls. In other words, what you see in the viewfinder may look much different from what your camcorder is seeing. Therefore, it's always a good idea to make a test recording of the scene and play back the videotape on a VCR that is hooked up to a TV set.

After you've reviewed the scene on a color TV set, you can make any necessary corrections to the lighting. Ask yourself these questions:

- Is this the kind of light I want on the subject?
- Are there shadows?
- Are the shadows falling where I want them?
- Do I want them to fall somewhere else?
- Is there enough light to faithfully reproduce the scene?

Sound

Sound is an important element in video-making, but one that most people tend to minimize. Camcorders come with a built-in microphone, usually located on top of the zoom lens. These microphones pick up sounds close to the mike very well—such as the voice of the camcorder operator, which is probably not what you want to record on the sound track of your video!

Built-in microphones pick up poorly sounds that are far away from the camcorder. If you try to record the sound of someone talking far away, the person's voice will sound hollow. Yet the *ambient*, or background, sound will be very loud. The built-in automatic gain control will make matters worse by raising the recording volume in an attempt to "hear" the person speaking. All it will

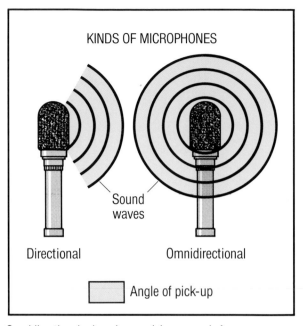

Omnidirectional microphones pick up sounds from all around, while directional mikes pick up sounds coming from one direction only.

accomplish is to turn up the volume of the ambient sound.

You can do two things to compensate for sound problems in your camcorder. First, get as close to your subject as possible. This will improve the recording quality of the person's voice and reduce ambient sound. Second, you can use a remote microphone, one that is detached from the camcorder. You can place a remote microphone close to the subject, even though the camcorder may be far away.

Microphones come in two basic types, directional and omnidirectional. The microphone on your camcorder is probably omnidirectional, which means that it picks up sounds coming from all directions. A directional mike, on the other hand, picks up sound from a specific direction. Sounds coming from another direction are ignored or minimized. If you choose to use a remote microphone, make sure it is directional.

Chapter Eight

TECHNICAL PREPARATION

If you are prepared for anything, you won't be disappointed. Nothing is more disappointing than having your shoot plagued with technical problems. While unforeseen problems almost always occur, there are some things you can do to minimize the unexpected and avoid disaster.

Care and Maintenance

Treat your equipment with respect and it won't let you down (most of the time— remember Murphy's Law!). Even with the best of care, your equipment will eventually require maintenance or fixing. If you treat your equipment roughly, or store it improperly, you're asking for trouble.

To be safe, pack your equipment in a protective case and keep it out of harm's way. Camcorders, batteries, videotape, and lenses can be damaged by heat, cold, humidity, dust, or rain. On a summer day, the inside of a car can get hot enough to melt plastic. If you must leave your equipment in a car, store it in the trunk and park the car in the shade. If you can, put the equipment case in a picnic cooler, which provides additional insulation from heat and cold.

Hot, humid climates present special problems for camcorders. If you store your equipment in an air-conditioned room and then take it outside, you must allow time for the equipment to adjust to the temperature difference. The hot, moist air will cause moisture on the equipment—especially the lens—to condense. Wipe off the lens and camcorder with a clean, soft cloth before using them.

Cold climates also present problems for camcorders. Batteries lose much of their charge in cold weather. When you're shooting in temperatures below 32° F (0° C), do not expect the battery charge to last as long as the manufacturer's warranted time. Also, the gears that control the auto iris and auto focus will strain to work in cold temperatures, because the oil that is used to reduce friction in these components will thicken.

When you're shooting in the rain, protect the camcorder with a waterproof covering. A large plastic garbage bag works very well for this purpose. Cut a hole in the bag large enough for the lens to poke through. In dusty conditions, the camcorder should also be protected by a waterproof/dustproof bag.

Lens Cap and Batteries

Always cap, or cover, the lens when not shooting. A lens cap protects the glass on the end of the lens from scratches, bugs, and other things that could hurt it. For additional protection, you may want to consider buying a *UV filter*, an attachment that reduces the amount of ultraviolet light entering the lens. It's far cheaper to replace a scratched filter than a lens.

Always charge the camcorder battery before a shoot—and immediately after a shooting session. If you can, carry a fully charged spare battery as well.

Sharing Equipment

When you use equipment that is owned by a school, club, church, or other group, make sure it works *before* you leave the equipment room. If it doesn't, you can report any problems to the person in charge and not be held responsible (and save yourself the embarrassment of not having your equipment work). Return the equipment in the same condition it was in when you received it. If there is a malfunction or damage, report it to the person in charge so it can be fixed.

Checklist

Before your shoot, make a list of the items you need, and inspect the equipment case to make sure everything is there. Here is a list of basic equipment:

EQUIPMENT ITEM	NUMBER
CAMCORDER	1
MAIN BATTERY	2
CLOCK BATTERY	1
EXTENSION CORDS	4
TRIPOD	2
UNIPOD	1
VIDEOTAPE	6
REMOTE MICROPHONE	
SPARE BATTERY	
BATTERY CHARGER	
CONNECTING CABLES	
EQUIPMENT CASES	
EQUIPMENT BAGS	

Additional items might include a portable lighting kit with lights, stands, and spare bulbs, extra AC extension cords, 2-inch (5-centimeter) wide duct tape, several 2 x 3 foot (.6 m x .9 m) reflector cards, and special lens filters.

Chapter Nine

CREATIVE PLANNING

Transferring your ideas from the script and storyboards to videotape is a process filled with excitement, change, anxiety, and, sometimes, disappointment. To finish the project, you must be prepared, expect the unexpected, and be flexible.

Why? What looked good on paper just might not look good through the viewfinder. Or, due to a last-minute scheduling problem, what you wanted to do simply can't be done. It's not as bad as it sounds, though, especially if you approach the project with a positive attitude.

The best way to do that is to think of the script and storyboards as a recipe—but not the finished dish. The raw ingredients are the **footage**, or scenes you shoot. The final dish is the result of the **editing** you do with the scenes you shoot.

Preproduction Planning

No matter how simple your video production, there will be lots of things to remember and keep track of if things are to go smoothly. "What props do we need for Scene 4?" "Where is Carver Park?" "Who's bringing the lights?" are typical questions.

Preproduction planning, or "prepro," is the work you do before the start of the shoot. Prepro helps you organize many details into a manageable order. The first step in preproduction planning is to read the script. The script tells you how many actors and locations will be used and what props, equipment, and special effects you will need. The script helps you estimate the amount of time it will take to shoot the video.

Although prepro requirements vary with each production, there are some common

59

elements. These include crew selection (determining the kinds of jobs required for the production and who will do them), location scouting (searching for the best places to shoot the scenes), casting (selecting the actors), and developing a "breakdown," a detailed list of the scenes that are to be taped each day.

From the breakdown, you can prepare a daily production schedule. The schedule lists the information everyone involved needs to know about each day's work. A production schedule may include the following:

talent list	crew list
scene list	call times
location(s)	props/set dressings
equipment	transportation
special requirements	

Let's look at each of these items more closely.

Talent refers to the people in front of the camera—the actors or people being taped or filmed. The prepro sheet often lists the talent's names, addresses, and telephone numbers.

Crew refers to the people behind the camera—the director, camera operator, sound recordist, electricians (called "gaffers"), production assistants (called "P.A.s"), helpers (called "grips"), makeup artists, and others. In a small production, one person may be doing many jobs. In fact, for most of your projects, you may be the whole crew all by yourself. If you can, though, ask friends and relatives to help you with as many of the jobs as possible.

The *scene list* is a list of the scenes that are to be shot that day.

Call times are the times the talent and crew are "called" or required to arrive on the set or the location.

Location refers to the place or places where the scenes are to be shot. A location could be anywhere: the middle of the woods, a downtown street, or someone's house. *Always* scout or visit a location before showing up with the talent, crew, and equipment. When you decide on a location, get permission to shoot there from the owner of the property or from the right government agency if it's public property. The owner will appreciate your courtesy.

Wherever the location, the call sheet will give the address, instructions on how to get there (if transportation is not provided), a contact person (such as the owner), and a telephone number, if any, at the location.

Props/set dressings are items used to decorate a set. Props are usually small objects such as a purse, pen, or lipstick. Set dressings are usually larger items, such as curtains, wall hangings, or furniture. For an office scene, set dressings may include a telephone, typewriter or computer, desk pad, and staple gun. In a living room scene, they may include a couch, pictures, and plants.

Equipment refers to the technical equipment needed to shoot the scenes.

Transportation. Because people can get lost or stuck in traffic, it is a good idea for everyone—talent and crew—to travel to a location together. If one person is missing from the location, the entire production can come to a halt.

Special requirements are any unusual items that will be needed to shoot the day's scenes.

On the facing page is the production schedule for "Field Trip to Carver Park."

Alice Smith Elementary School

Daily Production Schedule

Story: 6th Grade Field Trip to Carver Park

	October 15
Shoot Day:	Angela Conklin and Steve Braun
Reporters:	Ms. Mason's 6th grade class
School Talent List:	Jim Gilbert, Naturalist @ Carver Park
Adult Talent:	Ms. Mason
Teacher:	Jenny Uglum-Camera, David Olson -Assistant
Crew List:	10:30 a.m.
Call Time For Crew:	11:30 a.m.
Call Time For Talent:	Carver Park, Hwy. 5 and Hwy. 169. Meet at Info. Office. Telephone: 639-4792
Location:	Scenes #1 through #12
Scene List:	Camcorder, Portable Lighting Kit, 3 AC extension cords, 2 camera batteries, 1 battery charger, 1 remote microphone
Equipment:	Notebooks, pencils
Props:	None
Special Requirements:	Provided from school.
Crew Transportation:	Provided from school
Talent Transportation:	Burgers after shoot
Crew and Talent Lunch:	

Production Budget

Production Item	Days To Be Used	Cost Per Day	Total Cost
			Free
Camcorder	1 day	$10.00	$10.00
Lighting Kit	1 day	$6.00 each	$12.00
Videotape	2 rolls		
Props			$2.50
Animal Food			$15.00
Lunches/Snacks		$15.00	
Admissions		Free	
Parking		$5.00	$5.00
Talent	2 days	Free	

Grand Total: $44.50

Budget

The budget is a very important part of pre-production planning. A budget is a list of every item necessary to make the video and the cost of each item. It is prepared after reading the script and doing a breakdown.

Above is the production budget for "Field Trip to Carver Park."

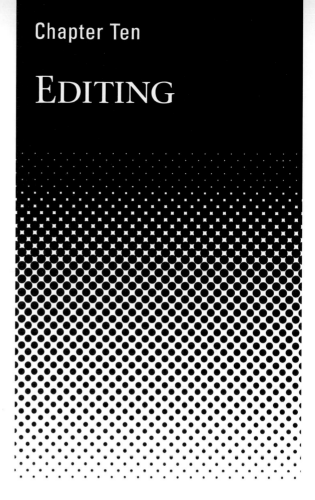

Chapter Ten

EDITING

Editing is the art of selecting the parts of scenes, the order of scenes, and the transitions between scenes that best tell your story. From a creative point of view, the possibilities are unlimited—and beyond the scope of this book. From a practical point of view, here are some techniques that will help you tell your story smoothly, without confusion or distraction.

Basically, there are two ways to edit the pictures and sounds into a finished video production: in the camera and electronically cutting and pasting.

In the Camera

This method ensures the best possible picture and sound quality. It is tricky to do well, because you can't change your mind about it later. In-the-camera editing begins with preproduction planning. If you know what scenes you are going to shoot and what's going to happen within those scenes, you can determine what you want to record and in what order. You *must* shoot the scenes in their chronological order. Rehearsing scenes is an excellent way of knowing what's going to happen before you "roll tape." It's also a good way for everyone to make suggestions for improving the scene.

While shooting, you edit by deciding when to end a scene. This is done by pressing the pause button on the camcorder. You decide when the next scene should begin by pressing the pause button again. Before pressing the pause button, you can do one of the transitional effects—if appropriate—such as swish pan, rack-focus, or fade-in/out shots. It helps to anticipate what's going to happen before it actually does. That, and practice, will help you get the hang of in-the-camera editing.

Below is an example of how "Field Trip to Carver Park" would look if we edited in the camera, using the camcorder's flying erase head to make seamless edits. There are two

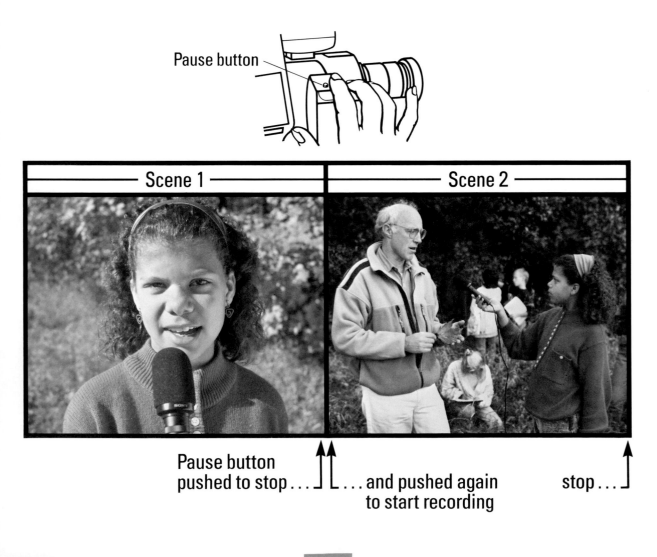

Pause button

| Scene 1 | Scene 2 |

Pause button pushed to stop . . . ⌐ └ . . . and pushed again to start recording   stop . . . ⌐

tricks to successful in-the-camera editing. The first is to shoot only as much of the scene as you need—no more, no less. This can be difficult, especially if you have little or no control over the action. Beginners tend to "shoot long," recording much more of a scene than is necessary to tell the story well.

The second trick is being able to *match action*. This means that the action and the relationship between objects in the frame are identical from a wide shot to a medium shot, or from a medium shot to a close-up. Shooting matched action requires the talent

to repeat the last part of the action of Scene 1 for the beginning part of Scene 2.

For the "Field Trip to Carver Park" report, we can find a good reason to use matched action. Scene 2 is a medium shot of Jim Gilbert holding leaves in his hand. Scene 3 is a close-up of those leaves. If we record a medium shot of Jim talking about the leaves, the scene could get too long. If we stopped recording to reposition the camera for the close-up of the leaves, by the time we were ready to continue shooting, Jim will have finished his talk.

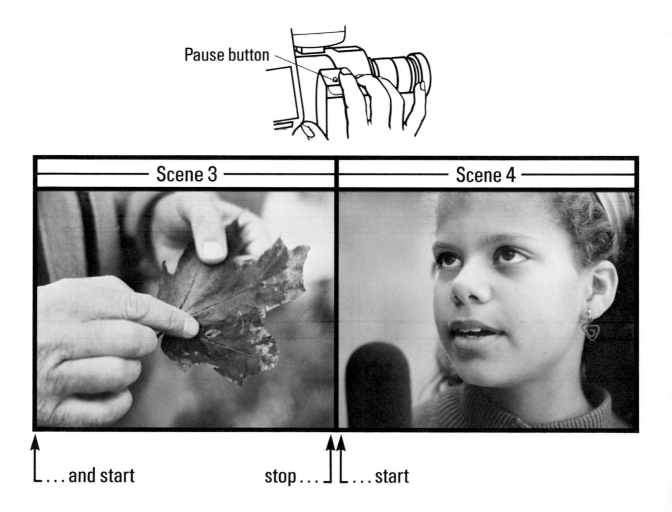

Pause button

Scene 3 Scene 4

...and start   stop... start

Cutaways

If you can't shoot matched action, you must shoot a *cutaway*. This shot "cuts away" from the action you've been looking at to something else. The cutaway is inserted between two scenes when there is no matched action—or when the action at the end of the scene is starting to drag. A cutaway should relate to the action—a reaction shot, for example.

The sequence below shows good use of a cutaway to improve pacing.

1) From this medium shot of Jim talking about the leaves, **2)** a cutaway shot moves to Angela and then back to **3)** a close-up of Jim.

Remember that in-the-camera editing means that the picture *and* the sound will stop and start when you press the pause button. You may have to let some scenes run longer than you want to allow a person to finish a statement.

Electronic Cutting and Pasting

The other kind of editing you can do is electronic cutting and pasting. It is much more complicated than in-the-camera editing, because you need to use at least two VCRs, preferably three, and specialized editing equipment. Three VCRs allow you to do "assemble" editing. Using electronic cutting and pasting also results in poor picture and sound quality, because you will be dubbing, or copying, your original recording onto another videotape. Any time you make a dub of a videotape,

the quality of the copy is diminished.

The finished production will be created on the VCR that is recording. By stopping and starting both VCRs, you can trim unwanted action from scenes and even change the order of scenes.

High-Tech Editing

Editing techniques and equipment for camcorder productions are becoming more sophisticated all the time. Technologies continue to emerge, making it easy to give your production a professional look. Video and computers can be used together by connecting your camcorder to a computer with a cable and a *video digitizer*. Some computer programs will let you superimpose graphics, titles, or animation onto a video image.

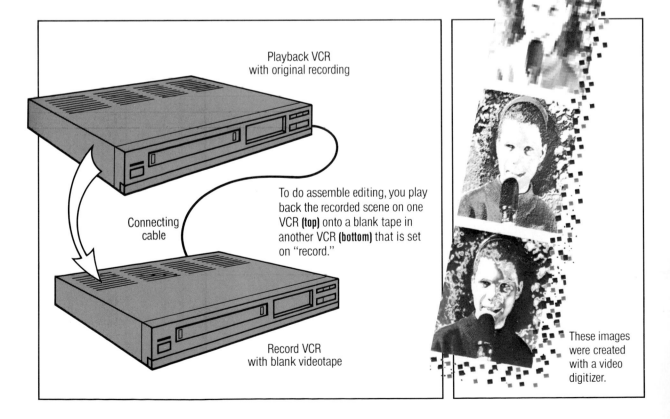

Playback VCR
with original recording

Connecting cable

To do assemble editing, you play back the recorded scene on one VCR **(top)** onto a blank tape in another VCR **(bottom)** that is set on "record."

Record VCR
with blank videotape

These images were created with a video digitizer.

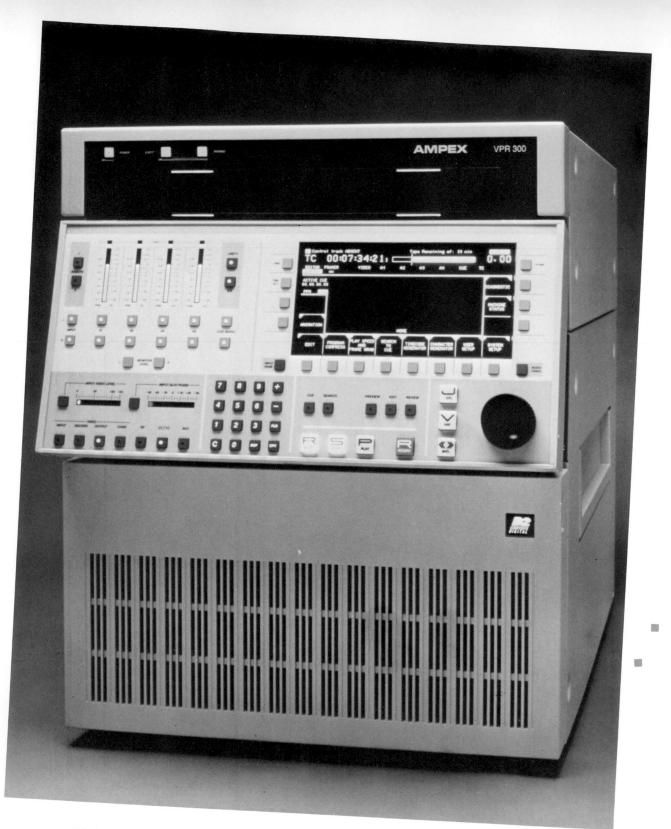

Television and video technology is constantly changing. This sophisticated digital videotape recorder is designed for television broadcasting.

THE FUTURE OF VIDEO TECHNOLOGY

Television has evolved and continues to change.

In video, the future is *now*! Changes and improvements in the world of television and video equipment are happening constantly.

It has been said that TV is a "window on the world." What began as a novelty more than 60 years ago has become one of, if not the most important means of communication. Yet the "tube" continues to change. As you read this, engineers and marketing people are working on new kinds of television systems that promise better picture and sound quality.

You can explore the world of video further by talking with your school's media specialist. He or she can direct you to more books and videos about videomaking. Perhaps your school offers classes in video production.

There are other resources you can take advantage of to learn more about video-making. In many communities, the cable TV system has public access channels available for everyone to use. Cable companies provide studios, equipment, and technical help for people to learn how to produce video and TV programs. In addition, community colleges, vocational technical institutes, scout groups, and schools often offer classes in videomaking.

While the technology and techniques used to communicate ideas change, the basic concept of a "good story well told" is timeless. There are many ways you can develop story-telling skills. Reading books is important. So is watching television and movies and observing how the video or filmmaker tells a story. In the end, the most important thing for you to know about making a video is to *have something to say and to know how to say it*.

Perhaps your school offers classes in video production, or you can learn at your local cable TV station.

aperture: the opening on the lens through which light enters the camcorder

aspect ratio: the size relationship between the height and the width of a rectangle

crew: the people behind the camera, such as director, camera operator, and electricians

cut: instantaneous change from one scene to another

depth of field: the distance between the nearest and farthest objects in focus in a frame

dolly: to move the camera closer to or away from the subject

editing: the selection and arrangement of video or film footage into the final product

focal length: a lens measurement that indicates the size of the image the lens creates

footage: the scenes of a video you shoot

frame: the outer boundary of what the camera sees

gain: the sound level or volume of what is being recorded by the camcorder

iris: an adjustable device that controls the amount of light entering the lens

jump cut: the editing together of two similar shots of the same person or action, with the subject in a slightly different position in each shot, so that the subject appears to abruptly move or jump from one part of the screen to another

lux: a measurement used to indicate a camcorder's sensitivity to light

pan: to move a camera horizontally

screen direction: the direction of the movement on the screen in relation to the camera

selective focusing: to focus on one object in a frame so that the rest of the objects in the frame are out of focus

shutter: a mechanical or electronic device that controls the amount of time a frame of film or videotape is exposed to light

shutter speed: the amount of time the shutter is open to expose film or tape to light

storyboards: thumbnail sketches of the important scenes from a video or film script

swish pan: a fast-moving pan that creates an intentionally blurry image

talent: the people in front of the camera—usually the actors

telephoto: a long focal length lens that creates large images of distant objects

tilt: to move a camera vertically

track: to move the camera parallel to a moving subject

white balance: a procedure a camcorder performs to make sure colors look "normal" under various lighting conditions

zoom: a lens that can change focal lengths to widen or narrow the field of view